THE TERRACOTTA ARMY OF EMPEROR QIN SHI HUANG

秦兵马俑

FOREIGN LANGUAGES PRESS BEIJING

外文出版社 北京

THE TERRACOTTA ARMY OF EMPEROR QIN SHI HUANG

People from all over the world who know even a little about Chinese culture, all admit that Emperor Qin Shi Huang was one of the most famous emperors in the 5,000-year history of China. He was born in 259 B.C., when China was undergoing a period of political reform and cultural prosperity. Showing his ambition when he was still a child, he succeeded to the throne of the State of Qin at the age of 13, and quickly threw himself into the work of reform. According to historical records, he was determined to unify China, a country divided into several rival states. He first turned Qin into a state of great prosperity and strength. Then, he led the powerful military forces at his disposal in a series of wars. It was not until 221 B.C. that he succeeded in wiping out the last of six rival states and establishing the Qin Dynasty, the first feudal dynasty in Chinese history to rule the entire country. He set up his capital, Xianyang, in Xi'an, Shaanxi Province, the center of the Central Plain culture. There he constructed the luxurious Epang Palace. Qin Shi Huang, like many other emperors in Chinese history, dreamed of immortality. He sent people across the East Sea in a vain effort to seek the fabled "elixir of eternal life." Immortality being beyond his grasp, in order to have a better life in the next world after his death, he started the construction of a stupendous mausoleum — a project that took 37 years to complete. It was a firm belief among the ancient Chinese that there was life after death in the nether regions, just as in the human world. The dead, therefore, were to be treated in the same way as the living. Emperor Qin Shi Huang was regarded as the supreme ruler of this world, and so he would remain in the next world. For this reason, his mausoleum, with its mountain-like tumulus and underground palace, was designed after the palace in Xianyang, where he lived and reigned. In addition, he was fully aware of the importance of armed force. He had images made of his troops and had them buried near him to guard his soul. The terracotta army was thus formed.

The Epang Palace was destroyed long ago, and we can only imagine the magnificence of the Qin Dynasty from historical records. However, archaeological finds help us to "go back in time." In March 1974, several of China's leading archaeologists gathered at a place 1.5 kilometers east of Qin Shi Huang's Mausoleum in Lintong County, Shaanxi Province, to excavate a 14,000-square-meter vault in which thousands of terracotta warriors and horses had remained entombed for over 2,000 years. Thus, the terracotta army, known as another "Wonder of Ancient Civilization," was brought to light.

When these warriors and horses were shown to the world, everybody was impressed by the fact that they were life-size as well as by their huge number. Subsequent excavation of the first, second and the third vaults made clear their formation and battle array. The first, second and third vaults are magnificent, covering an area of 20,000 square meters. They mainly contain infantry, cavalry and war chariots, serving as life-size reproductions of the Qin army of ancient China.

In those days, armies consisted of a legion of the left, a legion of the right, a legion of the center and the command headquarters. Vault 1 contains the barracks and enclosing walls of the legion of the right. It is rectangular, with the longer side lying east-west, and covers an area of 14,260 square meters. The floor of the vault is paved with blue bricks, while overhead the original roof was built of timber and covered with loess soil. The result was a large wood-and-earth underground structure with trenches. There are 6,000 terracotta warriors and horses in Vault 1. So far, some 1,000 warriors, eight war chariots and 32 horses have been excavated. The chariots are mingled with the foot soldiers, in a formation consisting of four parts: the van, the rearguard, the main body and the flanks. The battle formation in Vault 1 clearly places the light, flexible force in front, followed by the heavy and powerful force, to integrate the impact of assault with the solidity of backup troops.

Vault 2 contains the legion of the left. The array is shaped like a thick letter L, and consists of four small phalanxes. Phalanx 1, situated at the top of the L, forms the front corner of the whole formation. Phalanx 2, to the right of the base of the L-formation, is a chariot array composed of eight lines of eight chariots each, 64 in all. Phalanx 3, the middle of the L-formation, consists of three files of chariots reinforced by horses and foot. Phalanx 4 contains six chariots and 108 cavalrymen.

Vault 3, the command headquarter, contains the commanders' chariots. They are luxuriously decorated, and each has a general, a charioteer and a guard. The warriors in Vault 3 are the generals' bodyguards.

Most Western people wonder at the great numbers of the Qin warriors, and they feel puzzled at their stylized shapes. Actually, Qin figures are of high artistic value as sculptures of human figures, and are a landmark in the historical development of ancient sculpture in China. Although they may not be as vivid as the sculptures of the same period in the West, they emphasize the revelation of the subjects' inner world through their facial expressions and in a simple and vigorous style, characterized by a sense of a powerful internal force. The large numbers reflect the centralized authority in China's feudal society, serving as a typical example of different art of sculpture between East and West.

It is worth mentioning that there is individuality in the costumes and expressions of the warriors and horses. The Qin warrior figures show distinctive individual personalities, with different facial expressions. For instance, a face with a broad forehead, high cheekbones, thick brows, large eyes and stiff beard is the face of a hardy and fearless man, whereas a round face with regular features reveals a frank and open-hearted character. An oval face with fine features shows a genteel disposition. Then there is a square face with honest simplicity clearly written all over it. The young soldiers generally have chubby faces, and are smiling naively. The older soldiers, with lined foreheads, appear to be weather-beaten veterans who have seen much of the world.

Different costumes and hair accessories serve as distinctions of rank and position, including those of senior, intermediate and junior officers, as well as of soldiers with various arms and duties. In addition, the stances assumed by the men of different branches of the army are also different: Some are standing infantrymen, some kneeling archers, some standing archers, and some cavalrymen. All in all, they portray the military power of the Qin Dynasty, and are invaluable material for the study of the history, military affairs and culture of China over 2,000 years ago.

Qin Shi Huang, a great emperor in Chinese history, made a magnificent contribution to the development of the Chinese nation and its culture, and his underground army remains as a testimony to the splendor of ancient civilization in East Asia.

秦兵马俑

　　不论是东方人还是西方人，略通中国史的都承认，秦始皇是中华5000年中最有名气的皇帝之一。他诞生于公元前259年，那时的中国正处于一个政治变革、文化繁育又亟待整合的历史时期。他自幼即显现出远大抱负，年仅13岁便即王位，掌权后致力于文治武功。面对当时诸侯割据的局面，史书形容他"有席卷天下、包举宇内、囊括四海之意，并吞八荒之心"，在经过了一系列政治和军事运动后，终于在公元前221年歼灭六个诸侯国，建立了中国历史上第一个统一的封建王朝，自号"始皇帝"。他将国都设在中原文化的核心地区——西安地区的咸阳，在那里建造了庞大而奢华的宫殿"阿房宫"。秦始皇像中国的许多皇帝一样，一直幻想长生不老，曾多次派方士到海上去寻找仙药，结果无功而返，只得把全部希望寄托于好好安排冥世生活上，于是开始了长达37年的陵墓修筑工程。按中国古代的传统观念，人死是到阴间过另一个世界的生活，所以，对待帝王要"事死如事生"。秦始皇生前是一个至高无上的统治者，因而死后埋葬的陵园的建筑布局，也要模拟其生前宫室的形制。同样，因为他深知军队的重要性，所以必须要把军队的形象再现于地下，以护守亡灵。秦始皇陵兵马俑，就是在这种情况下诞生的。

时光荏苒，千年之后的今天，雄伟壮丽的阿房宫早已灰飞烟灭，当我们只能钩沉于史书来想象秦王朝的磅礴气魄时，考古的灵光却一再闪现。1974 年 3 月，中国权威考古学者纷纷聚集到陕西省临潼县秦始皇陵东侧1.5公里处，随即发掘出了超过1.4万平方米的兵马俑陪葬坑，以及数千件陶俑、陶马等文物，从而发现了在世界考古史上前所未有、被誉为"古代文明史上的伟大奇观"的秦始皇陵兵马俑。

　　当这些兵马俑陆续展现在世人眼前的时候，首先令人惊叹的是它酷似实物的比例和达到极至的个体数量。2000 多年前，一位伟大的中国皇帝用这种方式把他的"军队"带到了地下，使人们对他所存在的历史环境和个人韬略生出种种遐想。在随后的考古中，1 号坑、2 号坑、3 号坑和因某种原因未完成的一方俑坑陆续被挖掘、探定，秦俑的编队与战阵形制也逐渐清晰起来。其中1、2、3号俑坑形制宏伟，总面积达 2 万平方米。其内容主要表现的是秦始皇的步兵、骑兵和战车军阵，是中国古代庞大的帝国军队的一个真实缩影。

　　按中国古代兵阵法则，正规军队分左军、右军、中军和指挥部，1 号坑正属于右军营垒。这个平面呈东西向的长方形坑，占地面积达 14,260 平方米。它的底部以青砖墁铺，顶部搭建有棚木并覆盖黄土，是坑道式的土木结构的地下建筑。坑内是步兵俑、战车等，共有兵马俑6000 余件，目前已出土的有武士俑千余件，战车 8 辆，陶马 32 匹。是战车与步兵的混合编组，由前锋、后卫、主体、侧翼组成。前锋的排列为轻捷的手持弓弩的勇士在前，重装的武士居后，其后是战车与步兵相连的大型纵阵。其形制严整、规范，充分反映了中国兵法的列阵原则和军事思想。

　　2 号坑是相当于"左军"的军阵，它的结构为曲形阵，由四个小阵有机组合而成。第一个小方阵是弩兵阵，位于曲形阵的前端，构成军阵的前角。第二个小方阵为车阵，位于曲形阵的右侧。由 8 列共64辆战车组成。第三个方阵是战车和步兵骑兵相结合的纵阵。第四个是骑兵阵，由 6 辆战车和 108 个骑兵组成。

3号坑根据出土的内容来看，是军队的中心指挥部，出土战车为装饰华丽的指挥车，上坐将军、驭手和侍卫，而周围护卫的武士，就相当于现在的警卫队。

　　当西方人首次接触中国的秦兵马俑时，往往惊叹于它的个体数量，同时对它严谨而规范的形体表达表示不解和遗憾。其实，在中国古代雕塑的历史发展过程中，秦俑作为人体雕塑的艺术价值不容忽视。它与同期的西方人体艺术相比较虽然缺乏灵动的一面，却准确体现了富有东方特色的抽象与具象相结合的特征，庞大的数量体现了当时中国封建社会中央集权的权威性和皇权至上的审美追求，是东方雕塑艺术区别于西方雕塑艺术的一个典型范例。而从细节上来讲，兵马俑从服饰到表情又在规范中生出千变万化，令观者赞叹不已。

　　从秦俑的面部形象来看，数千武士面貌各不相同。有的是长方面庞，宽宽的额头，高高的颧骨，粗眉大眼，性格刚毅勇猛；有的面庞圆润丰满，五官端庄，胸怀豁达，性格爽朗；有的是椭圆形面庞，五官清秀，气质文雅；有的面庞方正，容颜浑厚，性格憨直。年轻的战士面带稚气；中年武士则面容苍老，饱经风霜。

　　从秦俑的服饰上看，它以各异的衣冠与头饰划分出不同的身份和职位，包括高级、中级和低级军吏和一般兵士。另外，各军俑依不同的军事职能，姿态也在统一中求变化，有直立俑、跪射俑、立射俑、骑兵俑等。这一切生动地再现了2000多年前的秦王朝的军事力量与配备，使今天的人们不仅把它当作一件举世罕见的艺术品，也作为古代的历史、军事、文化载体来进行各项重要研究。

　　秦始皇是中国历史上一位伟大的帝王，他对于中国文化的发展作过一些好事，也作过一些坏事，但无论如何，他倾力建造的这支庞大的"地下军队"，在两千多年以后已成为博大精深的东亚中原文明的智慧显现，虽然他未必愿意让它们这样重见天日。

Emperor Qin Shi Huang.
始皇帝像

Emperor Qin Shi Huang (259–210 B.C.) was the first emperor of a feudal dynasty to unify China. He had conquered the six other rival states by the year 221 B.C., establishing a strong and united central government. He died at the age of 50 on Lishan Hill, Lintong County, Shaanxi Province. His mausoleum is gigantic: The mound originally stood 115 meters high and measured two kilometers in circumference. Many discoveries of important remains and relics have been made there over the past three decades. The picture shows the mound covering Emperor Qin Shi Huang's Mausoleum.

秦始皇（公元前 259 年—前 210 年）是中国历史上第一个统一的封建王朝的皇帝，他于公元前221年消灭了周边6个封建割据的诸侯国，建立起强大统一的中央政权。秦始皇于 50 岁时卒于陕西临潼的骊山，他的陵墓规模很大，陵山封土建成时高达 115 米，周长超过 2 公里。近年在秦陵周边不断有各种重要的遗迹和遗物被发现。图为秦始皇陵的陵山封土。

10

The vaults housing the terracotta army of Emperor Qin Shi Huang, located 1.5 kilometers east of his mausoleum in Lintong County, Shaanxi Province, consist of three large pits — now numbered 1, 2, and 3 — in the imperial necropolis. Their combined area is over 20,000 square meters. Found in them was a treasure trove of rare and beautiful relics, including pottery (terracotta) warriors and horses, and wooden chariots. The discovery has been hailed as the "Eighth Wonder of the World" and "The Most Spectacular Archaeological Find of the 20th Century."

秦始皇陵的兵马俑坑位于陕西省临潼县秦始皇陵东侧1.5公里处，是陵园地下建筑的组成部分之一。从1974年到1976年我国考古学者相继发现了秦兵马俑的三处坑道遗址，分别编号为1、2、3号坑。三个兵马俑坑的规模形制十分雄伟，总面积达2万余平方米，埋藏文物丰富多彩，以陶俑、陶马、战车为主，被誉为"世界第八大奇迹"和"二十世纪最壮观的考古发现"。

A view of the excavation site.
未经整理的堆满陶俑的挖掘现场

Archaeologists reconstruct terracotta warriors.
考古工作者在初步清理陶俑

Terracotta horses being unearthed.
刚刚出土的破碎的陶马

A terracotta warrior before restoration.
未修复的陶俑的特写

14

Terracotta warriors and horses being unearthed.
揭开尘封的历史，是一个让世界惊奇的发现

16

A view of Vault 1.
1号坑外景

Vault 1 was discovered in March 1974. After six months of exploration and trial digging, Vault 1 was found to be 230 meters long, east to west, and 62 meters wide, north to south. It was 4.5 to 6.5 meters deep from the present ground level, and covered an area of 14.260 square meters. There are 6,000 terracotta warriors and horses in Vault 1, which has been identified as representing the legion of the right.

1974年3月，1号兵俑坑首先被发现。经过6个月的勘探、试掘，发现1号坑东西长230米，南北宽62米，距地面深4.5-6.5米，占地面积达14260平方米，里面埋藏着略大于实物的陶俑、陶马6千余件，根据古代作战"左军、右军、中军、指挥部"的军阵排列原则，1号坑应为战阵中的右军。

Soldiers of the battle formation of Vault 1.

1 号坑内整齐排列的军队，望之似可闻旌旗号角之声。

19

◁ Earthen partition walls were built in each pit to separate the rows of warriors, making every battle array independent.

武士的纵阵之间有夯土墙相隔，使每个纵阵成为相对独立的单元。

The chariots were arranged in mixed compositions with the foot soldiers, composing a rectangular formation facing east. Each array consists of four parts: the van, the rearguard, the main body and the flanks.

战车与步兵混合编组，排成一个坐西朝东的长方形军阵，由前锋、后卫、主体、侧翼四部分组成。

The life-size terracotta warriors, in huge numbers, are true-to-life models of the powerful army of the first empire of ancient China.

酷似实物的比例和极至的个体数量的陶俑, 是中国古代帝国军队的一个真实缩影。

24

Battle formations in Vault 1.
"整装待发的军阵"

In the summer of 1976, a second vault of the terracotta army was discovered 20 meters north of the eastern end of Vault 1. The L-shaped pit is 124 meters long from east to west and 98 meters wide from north to south, covering an area of 6,000 square meters. Trial digging indicated that buried in this vault were 89 wooden chariots and over 1,300 terracotta warriors and horses. The general layout in Vault 2, just as in Vault 1, is like a thick letter L, and consists of four small phalanxes of archers, chariots, chariots reinforced by horse and foot troops, and cavalry. The picture is an external view of Vault 2.

1976年夏，在1号兵马俑坑的东端北侧相距20米的地方，又成功发现了2号俑坑。其平面呈曲尺形，东西长124米，南北宽98米，面积约6千平方米。通过试掘得知，2号坑内有木制战车89乘，陶俑、陶马1300余件。2号坑内的兵俑列队为曲型阵，由4个小阵有机结合而成。第一个方阵为弩兵阵，第二个为车阵，第三个为战车、步兵、骑兵相结合的混合阵，第四个为骑兵阵。图为2号坑外景。

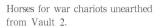

Horses for war chariots unearthed from Vault 2.

2 号坑内战车用马俑

28

Rows of infantrymen in battle formation in Vault 2.

2 号坑内的步兵俑

A terracotta charioteer of Vault 2.

2 号坑内的御手俑

Following the excavation of Vault 2, the archaeologists discovered the third pit of the terracotta
army to the north of the western part of Vault 1.
The plane figure of Vault 3 is in the form of the
letter U, measuring 17.6 meters long from east to
west and 21.4 meters wide from north to south.
Inside the pit are a wooden chariot and 72 terracotta
warriors and horses. Vault 3 served as the command headquarters. The picture shows a scene of
Vault 3.

在2号坑发现不久，考古工作者又在1号坑的西端北
侧，勘探出了3号兵马俑坑。3号兵马俑坑的平面呈
"凹"字形，东西长17.6米，南北宽21.4米，形制较
1、2号坑为小，出土木制战车1辆，陶俑、陶马72
件。此坑推测其功能为战略指挥部，主要为接见军吏
和办理军务之处。图为3号坑外景。

An interior view of Vault 3.
3号坑的局部排列

32

A panoramic view of Vault 3.
3号坑内部全景

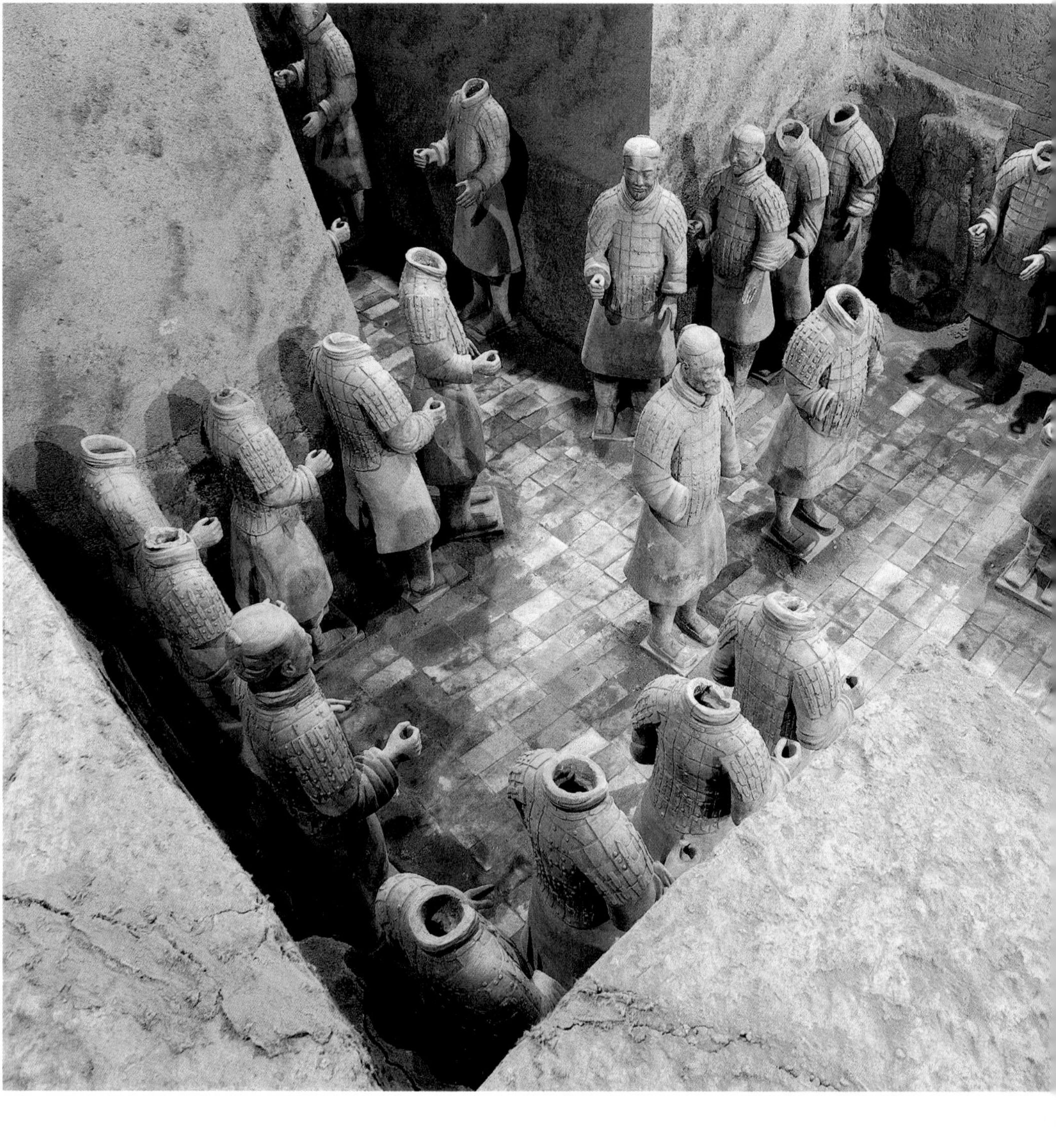

The southern hall and terracotta horses of Vault 3.
3号坑内的"南厢房"和陶马

Veins on the bronze chariot.
铜马车的车身上的精细花纹

 36

A number of rare and exquisite bronze chariots and horses unearthed from the eastern side of the vault is witness to the sophistication of the bronze-casting techniques of the Qin Dynasty. The picture shows the No.1 and No.2 bronze chariots and horses.

兵马俑坑东侧出土的一系列罕见的精致的铜车马，成为当时精湛的青铜铸造业的见证和象征。图为编号为1、2号的铜车马。

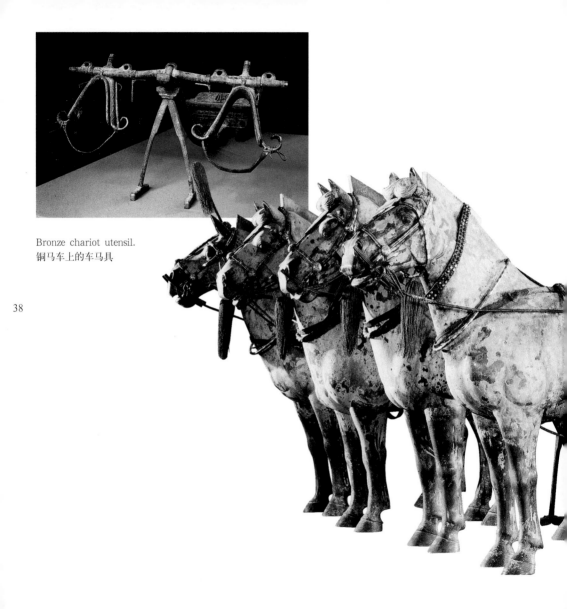

Bronze chariot utensil.
铜马车上的车马具

38

The No.2 bronze chariot and horses.
2号铜车马

41

The charioteer of the No. 2 bronze chariot and horses (front and back).

2 号铜车马上的铜御官俑
（正背面）

The Qin terracotta figures are remarkable for the characterization of their different ranks, occupations, ages, physical conditions and nationalities, as highlighted by their expressions, costumes, hairstyles and other features. The picture shows the head of a terracotta general.

秦俑的塑造各具情态，从服装、头饰、面貌等诸多方面反映了兵俑的职务、等级、年龄、体格、民族的差别。图为将军俑头部特写。

42

43

A terracotta general's hand ges-
ture and back view.

将军俑的手部和背部特写

44

A typical terracotta general.

将军俑

Head of a terracotta warrior.
战袍士兵俑头部

A terracotta cavalryman in armor.
骑兵俑

Kneeling terracotta archers (front and back).
跪射俑（正背面）

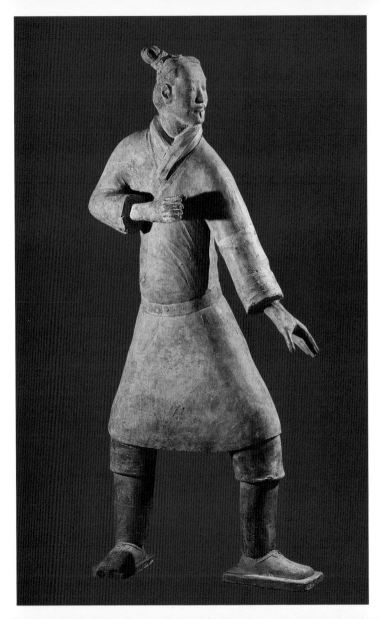

50

A terracotta archer in
a standing position.

立射俑

The original colors still stain the face of a terracotta warrior.
面部残存彩绘颜色的袍俑

52

◁ A terracotta officer wearing
a cap indicating his rank.

头戴长冠的军吏俑

53

A terracotta armored warrior.

铠甲俑

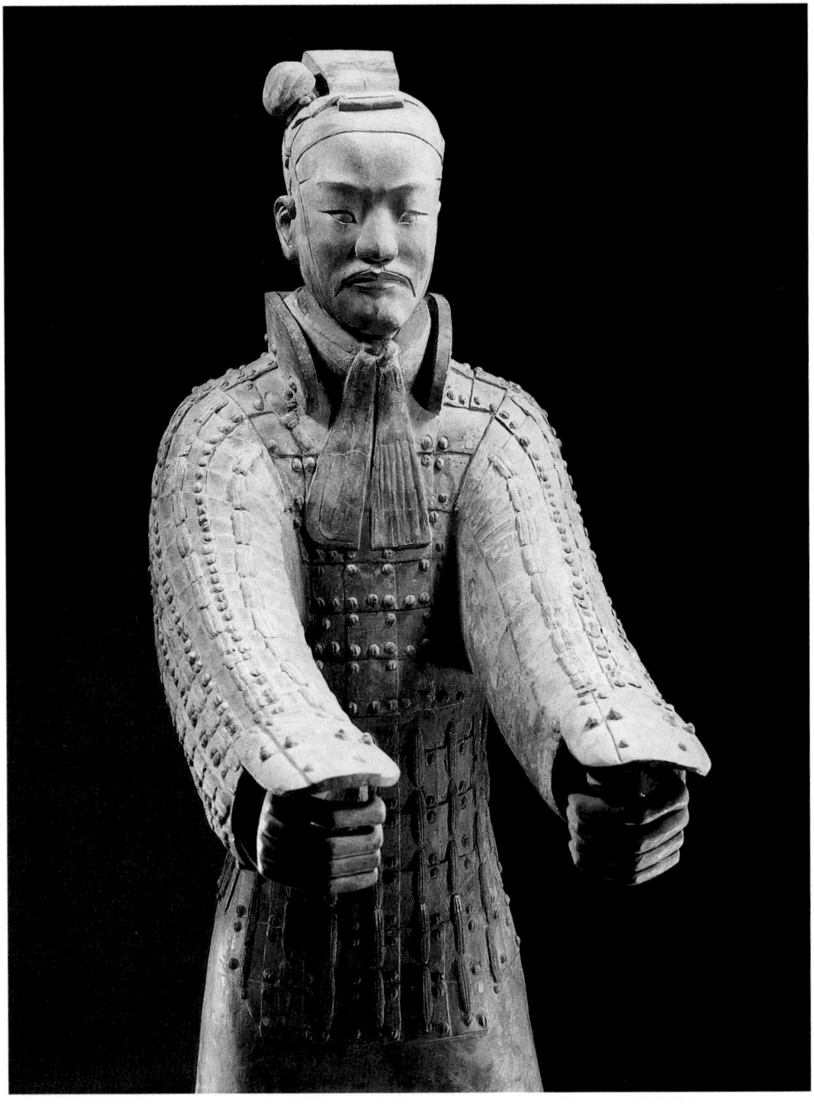

◁ A terracotta charioteer.
御手俑

A terracotta warrior.
士兵俑

The terracotta warriors are depicted in vivid detail, even including differences in height, weight, and personality.

仔细观察可以发现，兵俑的面部特征被刻画得细致入微，栩栩如生。不但高、矮、胖、瘦不同，而且个性气质也迥然相异。

Ethnic groups too are represented among the terracotta warriors.

制作陶俑的工匠在形态塑造中, 还注意了民族的差别。

59

The peoples of the western and northwestern areas of China are clearly depicted among the terracotta warriors.

有些陶俑的面目明显带有西域或西北地区的特征。

Different hand gestures of terracotta warriors.
兵俑们的手势塑造逼真，形态各异。

62

Remains of a wooden wheel of a chariot.
车迹

The details of the terracotta horses are anatomically correct, showing the important role that horses played in the life of the people of that time.

工匠对马的形体把握极其准确和精当，十分符合解剖学上各个部位的比例，从一个侧面说明当时马匹在人们生活中的熟悉程度和重要地位。

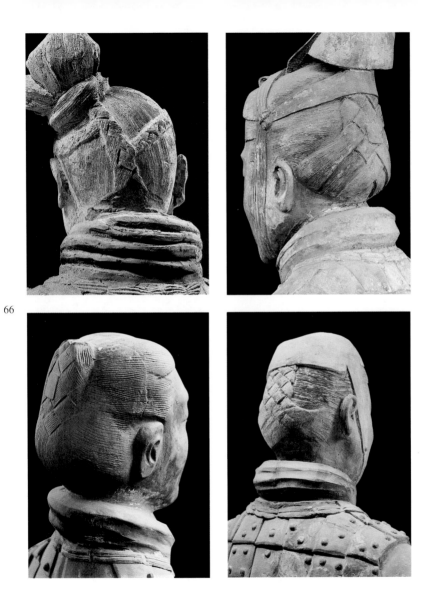

The diverse hairstyles of the terracotta warriors indicate an interest in personal adornment in ancient times.

兵俑的发髻表现形式多样，真实地再现了当时人们的装饰趣味，充满现实主义的创作魅力。

Various ancient weapons unearthed from the vaults.
兵马俑坑中出土种类和数量众多的古代兵器

A large number of bronze wares were unearthed during the excavation of the terracotta warriors, including weapons, insignia and daily utensils. The picture shows a bronze tiger, used as a token of command.

与兵马俑同时大量出土的还有各种青铜器，其中以兵器为主，也不乏珍贵的生活用器。图为古代军中指挥军阵用于命令的"虎符"。

Coins used during the Qin Dynasty.
秦朝流通的货币 "秦半两钱"

图书在版编目(CIP)数据

秦兵马俑／曹蕾编撰；夏居宪等摄影。－北京：外文出版社，2000
ISBN 7-119-02612-7

Ⅰ.秦…Ⅱ.①曹…②夏…Ⅲ.秦始皇陵－兵马俑－摄影集 Ⅳ.K878.9-64
中国版本图书馆 CIP 数据核字(2000)第 05627 号

Text by: Cao Lei
Photos by: Xia Juxian, Meng Zi,
           An Keren, Luo Zhongmin
           and Yang Limin
Translated by: Ren Ying
Edited by: Lan Peijin
Designed by: Yuan Qing

编撰： 曹 蕾
摄影： 夏居宪 蒙 紫 安克仁
        罗忠民 杨力民
翻译： 任 瑛
责任编辑： 兰佩瑾
设计： 元 青

秦兵马俑

曹 蕾 编撰

First Edition 2000

The Terracotta Army of Emperor Qin Shi Huang

ISBN 7-119-02612-7/J·1532

© Foreign Languages Press
Published by Foreign Languages Press
24 Baiwanzhuang Road, Beijing 100037, China
Home Page: http://www.flp.com.cn
E-mail Addresses: info@flp.com.cn
                 sales@flp.com.cn
Printed in the People's Republic of China

© 外文出版社
外文出版社出版
（中国北京百万庄大街 24 号）
邮政编码 100037
外文出版社网址：http://www.flp.com.cn
外文出版社电子邮件地址：info@flp.com.cn
            sales@flp.com.cn
深圳麟德电脑设计有限公司电脑制版制作
天时印刷（深圳）有限公司印刷
2000 年（24 开）第一版
2000 年第一版第一次印刷
（英汉）
ISBN 7-119-02612-7/ J·1532（外）
004800（精）